Food Science

Jeanne Miller

LERNER BOOKS • LONDON • NEW YORK • MINNEAPOLIS

Special thanks to Anna Rose for round-the-clock input; to Sue Corbett, Margaret Dubois, Jane Freeman, Connie Goldsmith, Ann Manheimer, Connie Sutton and Glenys Thomson for wise guidance; to Calvin and Natalie Wright for expert scrutiny; and to Beni Siegel for ideas and laughs

First published in the United Kingdom in 2009 by
Lerner Books,
Dalton House,
60 Windsor Avenue,
London SW19 2RR

Website address: www.lernerbooks.co.uk

This edition was updated and edited for UK publication by Discovery Books Ltd.,
Unit 3, Watling Street, Leintwardine, Shropshire SY7 0LW

British Library Cataloguing in Publication Data

Miller, Jeanne, 1947-
Food science. - (Cool science)
1. Food industry and trade - Juvenile literature
I. Title
641

ISBN-13: 978 0 7613 4297 7

Printed in Singapore

Table of Contents

Introduction

 id you know that

. . . a machine called MSNose helps a sweet company make new flavours?

. . . chocolate and fish eggs go together like crackers and cheese?

. . . cattle, pigs, chickens and insects can team up to feed one another – and you?

. . . drinking through germ-filled straws may help you live longer?

. . . in Japan, ducklings do the farming while their owners reap the rewards?

Welcome to the world of food science. This world is full of people looking for new ways to make healthy, tasty and convenient packaged foods.

It's a big challenge. Packaged food has to stay fresh while it sits in warehouses and shops, and it has to tempt us to buy more.

There's a lot more to food science than that though. This world also includes people exploring the changes that happen in cooking. They ask, 'What happens to food molecules when the food is heating'?

Food scientists work out how to make fast, convenient and delicious packaged foods. They also study farming practices.

A molecule is the smallest possible portion of a substance. Everything is made of molecules.

Restaurant chefs have joined the exploration too. Their discoveries help them create new dishes that surprise the senses. Food science helped one chef invent a bacon-and-egg ice cream that his customers love!

Food science can help food growers as well as food makers. Farmers use it to grow more food with less pest-killing and weed-killing chemicals.

We've come a long way from our early human ancestors, who hunted and gathered everything they ate. Step into this new food world, and take a look around.

chapter 1

A Matter of Taste

A manager at the Whiz-Bang Sweet Factory decides to make straw-berry-flavoured gob stoppers. He's going to fill them with a sour fizzing powder. He calls a flavour laboratory and describes the taste he wants: When people eat the gob stoppers, it reminds them of strawberries. It tastes sour and sweet and tickles the tongue.

At the flavour laboratory, Dr Caramel's shelves hold hundreds of bottles of liquid. Each liquid smells familiar – maybe a little like green apple, butter, almond or even grass.

These liquids are flavourings used by flavourists to enhance or re-create certain tastes.

Dr Caramel is a flavourist, a scientist who makes and mixes chemicals to create flavourings for foods. She's also a bit of an artist. She mixes flavour molecules the way a painter mixes colours to get the right blend. It may take her weeks to create the perfect flavour for Whiz-Bang's new sweet.

The Basic Five

A flavourist's work begins with understanding the human sense of taste. When you look inside your mouth, you can see little bumps on your tongue. Tiny taste buds are all over these bumps. Inside the taste buds lie even smaller structures called receptors. Each receptor waits for food molecules of a certain type to enter the taste bud.

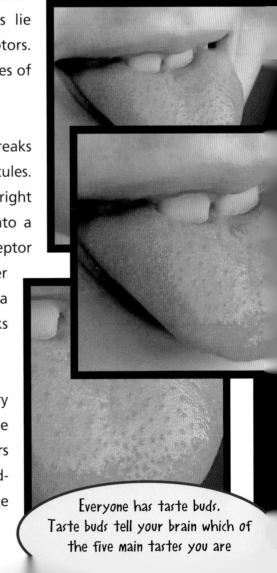

As you chew food, your saliva (spit) breaks down the food into separate molecules. When a food molecule reaches the right kind of receptor, it fits like a key into a lock. For example, a sweet taste receptor 'unlocks' only for sugars and other sweet chemicals. The receptor sends a signal to your brain. Your brain works out what taste is on your tongue.

Our tongues can pick up five primary tastes. (Primary tastes combine to make all other tastes, just as primary colours mix to create all other colours.) In addition to sweet, our tongues recognize sour, bitter, salty and umami tastes.

Everyone has taste buds. Taste buds tell your brain which of the five main tastes you are

What's umami? In 1907 a Japanese scientist named Kikunae Ikeda began wondering about the rich, savoury taste common to meat, fish, tomatoes and cheese. He named this taste umami. In 1908 he discovered it was due to the glutamate molecule. He even invented a seasoning based on this find. It's called monosodium glutamate (MSG). Ever since, cooks have been adding MSG to food for a richer flavour.

For years, nobody thought umami was a primary taste. In 2000, however, scientists discovered receptors on the human tongue that are sensitive only to umami. Unlike the other primary tastes, umami is a flavour booster. It makes food tastier, but it doesn't change the food's flavour.

The Nose Knows

A food's flavour comes from both its taste on your tongue and its aroma (smell) in your nose. How important is the nose in tasting? It can be even more important than the mouth. Try this: While holding your nose, put a fruit-flavoured sweet – maybe a lemon sherbert – in your mouth. Suck the sweet until you can taste its sweetness. Unplug your nose. How does the sweet's flavour change? Without your nose, you might mistake a sour lemon sherbert for a strawberry flavoured sweet!

Most foods have many different aroma molecules. As you chew, these molecules float from the back of your mouth up into your nose. They lock into some of the millions of receptors there. Like the taste receptors in your mouth, these odour receptors also send signals to the brain. Your brain reads the aroma signals from your nose and the taste signals from your mouth to tell you a food's flavour.

Working on Whiz-Bang's new sweet, Dr Caramel has to think about both your tongue and your nose. She needs to get the right balance of sour and sweet tastes and the right blend of aroma molecules. All together they should make your brain say, 'Strawberry'!

To match the taste of strawberries, flavourists have to blend the right sweet tastes and aromas.

Faking It

Luckily Dr Caramel has some amazing tools to help her. With two machines, a gas chromatograph (GC) and a mass spectrometer (MS), she can find out what flavour molecules are in a strawberry. Using the GC, she burns a sample of the fruit at high speed and high heat. As the fruit breaks down, it turns into a gas. Then the MS can identify each molecule in the gas. Now Dr Caramel knows all the molecules that make up a strawberry's flavour.

She can also use a machine called the MSNose to study the fruit's aroma. The MSNose examines air samples from a person's nose. Dr Caramel inserts a tube into her assistant's nose. Then she feeds him a strawberry.

IT'S A FACT!

Imagine you have one drop of the chemical that gives peppers their main flavour. You fill your town's swimming pool with plain water and mix in the drop. Could you taste it? Yes, you could. People are very sensitive to some flavours, and pepper is one of them.

Peppers contain a flavour chemical to which most people are very sensitive. Even a little bit of this chemical will make food taste like sweet pepper.

Hold the Cheese!

A British scientist used the MSNose to find out exactly how thick the cheese in a sandwich should be. He found that the cheesy aroma floating from his mouth to his nose got stronger as he added cheese. There was a limit to this effect, however. After a certain thickness, adding cheese didn't make the sandwich seem any cheesier.

So how thick should you slice your sandwich cheese for the cheesiest flavour? Cheddar cheese should be about 2.5 millimetres thick throughout the sandwich. Other cheeses may need to be thicker or thinner.

Making cheese thicker doesn't always make it cheesier. According to a British scientist, you stop tasting the extra cheese after 2.5 mm.

The numbers of aroma molecules floating from the assistant's mouth into his nose changes as he chews. The first ones to reach his nose are the ones on the outside of the strawberry. As he keeps chewing, the cells inside the fruit break open and free more and different molecules. (Cells are the tiny building blocks that make up living things. Many different molecules can exist in a single cell.) The MSNose tracks the changing number of molecules – and thus the changing aroma strength – in the assistant's nose from start to finish.

This flavour researcher is using a nasal sensor connected to a mass spectrometer, which is like an MSNose, to test the chemical reaction in his nose while he drinks orange juice.

About four hundred different aroma molecules eventually reach the assistant's nose. Dr Caramel uses about eighty of the most important ones to make her flavour recipe for Whiz-Bang's new sweet. Later, she tests her recipe with the MSNose. She compares her sweet test with her strawberry test. She makes sure the aroma molecules in the sweet rise and fall the same way they do for real strawberries.

Dr Caramel's strawberry flavour recipe for sweets is different than it would be for strawberry-flavoured muffin mix. Heat, cold and packaging change the flavour of food. For each different kind of food, she must find a different flavour recipe strong enough to keep its taste.

Beyond Good Taste

The fizzing powder inside Whiz-Bang's strawberry sweet is about fun as well as flavour. Some food chemicals excite a facial nerve that sends a pain message to the brain. For example, the heat of chilli peppers, the prickle of fizzy drinks, and the iciness of mints actually hurt a little. Most people enjoy this slight discomfort. It's part of the fun of eating certain foods.

An Important Partnership

Our tongues, our noses and our brains work together to bring us the delights of eating. Like cooks, flavourists work hard to make foods that please us. Their larders, filled with tiny bottles, don't look like the larder of chefs. The ingredients and the amounts may be different, but the end result is still a matter of taste.

chapter 2

The Science of Cooking

Imagine going to a restaurant and ordering a meal of rice, cauliflower and chocolate. After that, you have some apple-juice beads. Then, for dessert, you have bacon-and-egg ice cream. Would you believe that some of the most famous restaurants in the world actually serve these dishes?

The chefs at these restaurants work with scientists to understand how and why food appeals to customers. One result is new dishes with surprising flavours and textures. Another result is kitchens that look like labs!

This bacon-and-egg ice cream was made at a restaurant in Britain. It is served on a piece of French toast topped with bacon.

One chef opens his restaurant for only half the year. He spends the other half doing food experiments.

What Goes with What?

Studying the chemical makeup of individual ingredients leads to some strange food pairs. For example, one restaurant serves caviar (salted fish eggs) on a disk of white chocolate. This pairing works because caviar and white chocolate share many flavour molecules.

IT'S A FACT!

An engineer named Percy Spencer noticed one day that microwaves from a magnetron (a type of radar equipment) had melted the chocolate bar in his pocket. He experimented with popcorn and eggs. Both cooked very quickly. This discovery led him to invent the first microwave oven.

Flavourists have studied hundreds of foods. They keep lists of flavour molecules in these foods. Chefs can look at these lists to find what any two foods have in common. Chocolate and blue cheese, for example, share many flavour molecules. Bananas and parsley do too. If you tried eating one of these pairs, you might be surprised.

Not What You Expect

Surprising the senses is an important part of this new cooking style. It's fun to eat something that's unexpectedly tasty.

Most ice cream is made with eggs – but not bacon. A few years ago, a chef in Britain overcooked the egg custard for his ice cream. He noticed that the mixture tasted like scrambled eggs. He decided to experiment. He made his next batch of ice cream with roasted bacon, straining out the bacon bits before freezing the mixture. His bacon-and-egg ice cream has become a big hit. When you eat it, your nose tells you it's breakfast. Your eyes and mouth, however, tell you it's dessert.

Juice beads anyone? Some science-loving chefs mix apple juice with a tasteless chemical that comes from seaweed. They release drops of the mixture into a special chemical bath. A thin skin forms around the liquid centre of each drop. When you see a dish of these jelly-like beads, you might think they're caviar. But they don't smell or taste of the ocean. Instead, when they pop in your mouth, you get a burst of strong apple flavour.

Though surprising people with food is fun, it's also serious. The chefs are on a quest to understand each ingredient. They want to know exactly what happens when you mix them, freeze them, heat them and so on.

Browning Magic

Why does a roasting chicken smell so good? Because heat starts a chemical reaction called browning. During browning, proteins and sugars on the surface of a food combine to create new flavour molecules. Scientists don't yet understand every step of the process, but they know that browning different foods produces different tastes. Food scientists copy these new flavour molecules to create artificial flavours for foods.

Lots of cooking methods and rules have passed from cook to cook over the centuries. Most cooks follow these rules without hesitation. But some modern chefs ask, 'Why do we do it this way?' Answering that question may require machines not available to cooks of the past – and not usually found in restaurants.

One scientist scanned chips with a magnetic resonance imaging (MRI) machine. Doctors use MRI to look inside people's bodies. This scientist wanted to study the perfect chip (fluffy inside, crisp and brown outside, and not greasy). MRI showed that chips get soggy when oil enters tiny cracks in a fried potato's surface, but the oil gets in only as a chip cools. That's why restaurants drain the oil from chips when they're still hot.

Above is an MRI machine. It takes pictures of the insides of people's bodies. One scientist used MR discover what makes a perfect chip.

Chefs know that we experience food not just through taste and smell. Enjoying food also involves our senses of vision, touch and even hearing. That's why chefs arrange food artfully on plates. It's also why chefs pay close attention to texture.

For most people, eating a limp celery stick isn't as pleasant as eating a crisp one. Both celery sticks have the same flavour molecules, but a nice *snap* between our teeth appeals to our brain's touch and hearing centres. In a similar way, smooth, velvety ice cream seems more delicious than ice cream with gritty ice crystals in it. Crisp chips seem more delicious than soggy ones.

A Good Egg

Boiled eggs often have rubbery whites and crumbly yolks – both rather unpleasant textures. Most people cook whole eggs in boiling water. Water boils at 100°C. Scientist-chef teams have found that it's best not to fully boil a boiled egg.

What happens when you boil an egg? Its white and its yolk are like two bags of water with different kinds of balled-up protein molecules floating in them. As an egg heats, its proteins begin to unwind and connect

Brain Food

Humans have bigger brains than other primates (the group of mammals that includes humans, apes and monkeys). A scientist who studies chimpanzees believes he knows why. He thinks humans developed bigger brains after early humans began to cook their food. Cooking food makes it easier to digest. Easier digestion uses less energy.

Our brains are hungry organs. Over half the energy a newborn baby uses is for brain activities. A resting adult's brain uses a quarter of the body's available energy. Cooked food gives our bodies the same amount of fuel as uncooked food but for less effort. The energy we save by eating cooked foods can fuel our brains.

with one another. They create a network that captures the egg's water molecules. As the temperature rises, different proteins unwind and link up. If you heat the egg all the way to boiling, all its proteins get tangled up together. This makes the white tough and the yolk dry.

This egg was boiled the old-fashioned way, so its yolk is crumbly and its white is tough. Some scientists have worked out how to cook whole eggs without changing their texture so drastically.

Thanks to this new understanding of eggs, many restaurants proudly offer eggs cooked to exactly 65°C. That's not hot enough to tangle many of the proteins. These eggs have a delicate, custardlike white and a runny yolk. With the right equipment, eggs can stay at this temperature for hours. Even sitting at 65°C overnight, they stay soft. Any germs in the egg die after a few minutes at 60°C, so they're perfectly safe to eat.

Cooks have always been experimenters. Most cooks have tried to improve their dishes by making them in different ways. Some chefs simply take that challenge one step further. They use modern science to understand and control their ingredients. They want to offer new eating adventures. Their goal is making food that appeals to people's mouths, noses, eyes and brains.

Fake Food

hocolate bars, fizzy drinks, crisps . . . they're all junk food, but people love them anyway. What makes them junk food? Too much and too little! That's too much sugar, too much salt or too much fat and too little of the nutrients our bodies need to stay healthy, like protein, vitamins and minerals.

Why do people love junk foods? They taste good! Our bodies are built to love them. In small amounts, fats and sugars are a great energy source to fuel or warm our bodies. Salt gives us sodium, which we need to control some body functions. So what's the problem?

Junk food is everywhere. It's also cheap. It's easy to eat too much of it. When we fill up on foods like sweets and crisps, we're not hungry for healthy foods. Undernourished bodies are weaker and more likely to become ill.

Manufacturers are looking for ways to give us healthier forms of the sweet, salty and fatty tastes we like. Is it possible for foods that contain no sugar, salt or fat taste as if they do? That's what food scientists are trying to find out.

How Sweet It Is

Scientists have studied how we recognize the taste of real sugar. They've found that we sense its sweetness as soon as the sugar touches our tongues. The sweetness peaks and then clears, leaving no aftertaste.

The success of artificial sweeteners depends on how closely they match that experience. The first artificial sweetener, saccharin, is three hundred times sweeter than sugar. People use only tiny amounts of saccharin to replace sugar, but it still leaves a bitter aftertaste.

Many other sweeteners have followed: aspartame, acesulfame-K, sucralose and more. Each has drawbacks. Its sweetness may come on too slowly or last too long. It may

IT'S A FACT!

In 1879 a chemist sat down to dinner after a day at work. He picked up some bread and ate it. It tasted surprisingly sweet. He returned to his lab and tasted the chemicals he'd touched. Sure enough, one of them was sweet. It became the first artificial sweetener, saccharin.

These pills are actually tablets of aspartame.

taste bitter or metallic. If you eat too much of it, you might have to run to the lavatory.

Most makers of processed food (foods changed using technologies such as flavouring or freezing) find that combining artificial sweeteners works better than using them alone. For example, one gives a quick taste of sweetness, while a second masks the first one's bitterness. Blended in just the right amounts, they fool our brains into thinking we're tasting sugar.

Of course, there's more to sugar than sweetness. It gives bulk, tenderness, and moisture to baked goods. It stops jams from going off. It balances sour flavours. When food scientists skip the sugar, they have to add other ingredients to do sugar's many jobs.

A New Approach

One company is seeking a different way to sweeten foods. It's not looking for a sugar substitute. It's looking for a chemical that makes sugar seem sweeter.

This company's scientists use artificial taste buds to test lots of different molecules for sweetness. Each taste bud contains a cell with a sweet taste receptor. Robotic arms squirt various chemicals onto hundreds of taste buds. When a molecule locks into a receptor, the cell lights up. That means the molecule is sweet. Would it be good in food? More tests will decide that.

These scientists hope to find a molecule that will attach with sugar to the sweet receptors on our tongues. Using this chemical, cooks could make sweet dishes with less sugar. For example, 100 grams of sugar plus a drop of this chemical could replace 200 g of sugar.

Fooling Our Taste Buds

Imagine eating a strange red berry and then sucking on a lemon and finding it as sweet as a peach. This berry is real, and it comes from western Africa. It's called miracle fruit.

After the fruit coats your tongue, bitter and sour foods taste sweet. Scientists studying the fruit believe it has a protein that binds to taste receptors and changes them. The change usually wears off in two hours or less.

Miracle fruit isn't readily available in the United Kingdom, but it is in Japan. Japanese people who are trying to lose weight or who can't eat sugar for health reasons use the berry to satisfy their longing for sweets.

The top image shows a miracle fruit plant, and the bottom image shows miracle fruit berries close up.

The scientists are trying to do the same thing with salt. Our bodies need just a little of the sodium we get from salt. Too much salt can cause health problems. With a chemical that boosts the taste of salt, a bowl of canned soup could contain just one-third of the usual amount of salt.

One product that's already available acts like umami, boosting food's natural flavour. It can replace MSG, which contains sodium. Another new product can block bitter tastes. People who don't like brussels sprouts, water cress or other healthy but bitter foods might find them delicious with the help of a bitterness blocker.

Fake Fat

People are drawn strongly to fatty foods. Scientists wonder if fat gives food more than texture. Could there be a primary fat taste – and fat taste receptors? Studies suggest that rats have fat-sensitive taste receptors on their tongues. It's too early to know whether people do too, but scientists believe we might.

Like sugar, fat plays many roles in food preparation. Finding one substitute to do all those jobs hasn't been easy. The most successful attempt produced olestra. It acts like fat in cooking and in cold foods. It has zero calories because our bodies can't absorb it. It doesn't change as it travels through our digestive system (the stomach and organs that together break down food). Unfortunately, olestra also absorbs certain vitamins as it passes through us. Some users report stomach pains, gas and diarrhoea. Although a few snack foods contain olestra (plus added vitamins), many people are wary of it.

These crisps were made with olestra, a fat substitute that the human body can't absorb.

Other fat substitutes work in some foods but not all. As with sugar, the food industry usually combines many different ingredients to replace fat.

Food scientists may never be able to turn junk food into health food. But their efforts could create snack food that's a little better for us.

Wise Choices

Processed foods play an important role in modern meals. We can eat sweet corn all year long thanks to canning and freezing, and preparing bolognese using a bag of pasta instead of starting with flour and eggs saves hours! From breakfast cereal to tuna salad sandwiches, we rely on packaged foods for convenience and variety.

Health experts say that fresh whole foods and dishes made with natural ingredients are best. Processed foods have their place, but we must choose them carefully. Read the list of ingredients on the label. Can a snack cake with 32 ingredients be a healthy choice? Probably not.

Food companies sometimes use many artificial substances to replace one real one. They say they're just trying to make healthy food taste better and tasty food more healthy, and it also saves them money.

Will advances in food science lead to more fake food? Only time will tell.

chapter 4

Slowwww Food

It's 20 March 1986. At the edge of a famous square in Rome, Italy, a McDonald's opens for the first time.

A small group marches towards the restaurant. They're not coming for burgers though. They're coming to fight the fast-food invaders. Their weapons? Bowls of pasta, which they serve to passers-by.

The protesters know that their pasta bowls are no match for the golden arches. But they don't know that they're launching the international Slow Food movement.

Endangered Foodways

In the 1980s, the world of food was changing rapidly. Family farms were giving way to factory-style farms. Village grocery shops were closing as centralized supermarkets moved in. Small eateries serving traditional local fare were losing business to a giant restaurant chain. The protesters in Rome were worried. Italy was losing old varieties of fruits and vegetables. Some handmade Italian cheeses and sausages had disappeared. Italian food lovers decided to organize to stop the spread of factory-style food production. The Slow Food movement grew from this organization. A quarter of a century later, it has more than eighty-five thousand members around the world.

This movement is changing the way people think about food. It demands farming, food distribution and cooking methods that are good for our bodies, our communities and our planet.

Food Factories

When you imagine a farm, what do you see? Do you picture a house surrounded by gardens with rows of lettuce, tomatoes, beans and carrots? Chickens pecking at insects in the grass? Children playing in the farm yard? Kittens tumbling in the barn's hayloft? Cows grazing in nearby fields? Or do you picture hectares of single-crop fields, broken only by an occasional cluster of low warehouses? Not a house, person or animal in sight?

These children are feeding the cattle on their family's dairy farm.

This tractor is planting a massive field in the United States.

The farm you pictured first was common in your great-grandparents' time, but it's not anymore. Most modern farms are like the second picture. Slow Food members – and many other people – think something is wrong with that picture. They want to bring back the old-style farm, with its varied crops and livestock.

For centuries, farmers kept their soil healthy using simple, natural methods. They rotated their crops from field to field and mixed in their livestock's manure (animal waste) to add nutrients. Then in the 1950s, factory-made fertilizer became available. Along with pesticides to kill insects and herbicides to kill weeds, fertilizer changed the way farmers grew food. They no longer depended on natural relationships between crops and livestock.

IT'S A FACT!

A nutritionist in London tries to buy locally grown food. She worked out that shipping one strawberry, for example, from the United States uses over 400 calories of fossil fuel. But that strawberry gives her body only 5 calories of fuel when she eats it.

Most modern farms are like factories. They specialize in one or two products. A chicken farm houses thousands of chickens, crowded into cages or warehouses. On pig farms, the animals spend their lives in tiny indoor pens, gaining weight until butchering time. Farms might grow hectares and hectares of wheat or barley but have little or no livestock.

The Hidden Costs

After farming chemicals became available, their use spread quickly. When a farmer applied artificial fertilizer, the land produced more food. Pesticides allowed farmers to plant all their land in a single crop. This made tending it more efficient. Weeding had been time-consuming but herbicides killed weeds for good.

More food with less labour: it seemed like the answer to the world's problems. Over time, however, we have seen the drawbacks of this kind of farming.

Making fertilizer, herbicides and pesticides takes a lot of fossil fuel (oil, coal and natural gas). It takes even more fuel to transport and apply all those chemicals.

Farming chemicals get into streams, rivers and groundwater (underground water that supplies wells and springs). This polluted water harms wildlife and people. For example, in the US the Mississippi River carries rain runoff from midwestern farms into the Gulf of Mexico. This has created a dead zone 20,000 square kilometres (8,000 square miles) wide where the river meets the sea. No sea life can survive there.

Pesticides and herbicides are powerful poisons. Many of them cause cancer and birth defects. Farm workers who have to handle them risk serious illness.

Factory-style farming causes other problems too. Throughout human history, more than three thousand food crops have fed us. But in the early twenty-first century, just eight crops provide 75 per cent of the world's food. Imagine what would happen if one or more of these crops failed.

Locavores

There is a growing concern about the distance that certain foods have to travel before they reach our supermarkets here in the United Kingdom. Of course being able to buy the same foods all year round, rather than having to wait until they are 'in season' is great, but what about the environmental costs? Getting foods from all over the world consumes lots of resources, particularly fuel, and this is bad for the environment.

Can you be a locavore? Try not eating anything that's travelled more than 160 km (100 miles). For example, choose apples from a local orchard, not those from another part of the world. They'll be fresher and they'll have used a lot less fuel and other chemicals getting to you.

Disasters like that have happened before. In the mid-1800s, potato blight (a fungal infection) destroyed Ireland's main food crop. About 1 million Irish people starved to death.

In the 1970s, a disease destroyed rice fields across Asia. Scientists searched for a rice plant that could resist the disease. Four years later, they found it growing wild in India. Growers mated it with other rice plants. The wild Indian rice saved the world's most important food crop.

Growing identical crops on more and more of the world's farmland carries great risks. Crop variety helps protect our food supply. It ensures that disease-resistant plants survive to replace their sickened relatives.

Out with the New, in with the Old

Some farmers are bringing back and improving old-fashioned farming. They call it biodiverse farming. A place that's biodiverse is home to many different kinds of living things. On a biodiverse farm, a variety of plants

Free-Range Eggs

People practising biodiverse farming can't keep up with the demand for free-range eggs. These come from chickens that are allowed to roam 'free' in fields and farmland. Luckily, modern farmers have electrified plastic netting — a handy tool their great-grandparents lacked. This lightweight fencing makes temporary chicken pens easy to set up. Not only are the chickens healthier, they also eat insects in the fields. So farmers can move chickens where they're needed most for pest control. Their diet of insects and worms produces delicious eggs with rich yellow orange yolks. Customers love them!

Biodiverse Farming – the Results

So what can a biodiverse farm produce in a year? With 40 hectares of cropland and 180 hectares of woodland – and no artificial chemicals – a biodiverse farm could produce:

30,000 dozen eggs	250 pigs
10,800 chickens	1,000 turkeys
50 beef cattle	500 rabbits

and animals share the land and help one another thrive. They also work together to keep the soil healthy.

Farmers move different kinds of livestock from field to field in carefully timed cycles. In each field, grasses take in minerals from the soil and use energy from sunlight to create sugars. Cattle eat the grass, getting the nutrients their bodies need. Their manure puts nutrients back into the soil. Then they move to a new field.

Three or four days after the cattle have left a field, the chickens come in. By this time, the maggots in the cow pats are fat, but they haven't yet grown into flies. The chickens find these grubs tasty. They pick them out and eat them, ridding the field of potential disease-carrying insects. These pests give the chickens free protein. The chickens' droppings put more nutrients in the soil, nourishing the grasses that will later feed cattle again.

Pigs in portable pens sometimes play a role too. They root around in the soil, which encourages grass seeds to sprout. Pigs help fields grow lush and thick.

In Asia, biodiverse farming includes raising ducks and rice together. After planting the rice seedlings, farmers release ducklings into the rice paddy (muddy, flooded field). The ducks gobble up insects and snails that eat the rice seedlings. The ducks also eat weeds. (Fortunately, they don't like rice seedlings.) They churn oxygen into the water as they dig up weeds, helping the rice grow. The ducks' droppings also enrich the muddy soil.

In other words, the ducks are doing the weeding, the ploughing and the fertilizing! The farmers get more rice with less work and fewer chemicals – plus ducks, eggs and ducklings at no extra cost.

This Vietnamese farmer tends his flock of ducks in a newly harvested rice field.

Feeding the World: Japan

Japanese rice farmer Takao Furuno experimented with growing ducks and rice together. He perfected the system on his farm and then began teaching it to others. Each year his 2 hectares of paddy fields and vegetable gardens produce:

- 6.5 tonnes of rice
- 300 ducks
- 4,000 ducklings
- enough vegetables for 100 people

Farming this way, just 2 per cent of the people of Japan could feed everyone in the country.

In biodiverse farming, animals live much healthier less restricted lives. They have plenty of space, fresh air and exercise. They peck and scratch and root out the foods their bodies need.

The Big Debate

Some experts think we can't produce enough food for the world's ever-growing population without using factory-made farm chemicals. Without artificial fertilizer, they say, a piece of land would produce much less food. They also worry that there wouldn't be enough natural fertilizers to replace all the artificial fertilizers used.

Other experts disagree. They point to a review of worldwide studies conducted in 2007. These studies compared the output of land farmed with herbicides and pesticides to the output of land farmed naturally.

The amounts were about the same overall. They also found that farmers could produce enough natural fertilizer for crops to thrive. In Japan, scientists have found that raising ducks and rice together actually multiplies the rice harvest.

Nature raises many species on the same piece of land. According to the latest research, that appears to be a good model for humans to adopt.

Foods of the Future

It's a day in the future and you're shopping for food. You stick a card containing your health details into a slot on the shopping trolley handle. As you walk down the aisles, the trolley sends information to the shop shelves.

The shelf labels for some items light up. Those are the foods best for your particular body. You choose salmon, broccoli, wholemeal bread, olive oil and Brazil nuts. The labels for some nutrient-enriched drinks are flashing. So is the label for drinking straws lined with friendly bacteria. (Bacteria are single-celled organisms sometimes called germs.) You add them to your trolley and move on to the check out.

You cycle home with your food. You can't remember the last time you were ill. It was definitely before you got that amazing nutrition card.

Is this science fiction? Not for long.

Food as Medicine

That's the promise of a new science called nutrigenomics. *Nutri* refers to nutrition and *genomics* to your genome. Your genome is the collection of all your genes. Genes provide your cells with the chemical recipes they need to keep your body working.

Your genes control your eye colour, your height and thousands of other traits. Half your genes come from your mother and half from your father. (If you're adopted, your genes are from your birth mother and father.) That's why you may look like your parents did when they were your age.

IT'S A FACT!

Once a mammal stops needing its mother's milk, it loses the ability to digest milk. About nine thousand years ago, some human societies began herding certain mammals. Over time, genetic change enabled these people to digest milk after childhood. If you can digest milk, these people were probably your ancestors.

Members of families look alike because they have many of the same genes. Genes control many human physical characteristics.

Genes don't always work properly. They may carry diseases from parent to child. For example, your genes could make you more likely to get heart disease or some kinds of cancer.

Scientists expect that in the future, most people will know exactly what genes they have. By that time, scientists will know a lot more about the role genes play in causing diseases. They'll also know much more about food chemicals that can affect genes.

A nutrigenomics lab will study your genome to see if you have genes that might make you ill one day. Then it'll look for foods that might help you. Using this information, the lab will prescribe you a personal eating plan. Eating the foods on your plan will help you avoid getting ill.

This geneticist is working on the Human Genome Project. This project is mapping the human genome. It could help make nutrigenomics a reality.

Nutrigenomic prescriptions are still a long way off, but many scientists are working hard to reach that goal. One day people may have less need for medicines. We'll improve our health with products from supermarkets instead of chemists.

Beyond Vitamins and Minerals

Every day we learn more about chemicals in food that help us stay healthy. For example, we've known for a long time that eating fish gives us protein. We recently found that fish also provides omega-3 fatty acids, which help prevent heart disease. We know yoghurt gives us protein and calcium. Modern science reveals that the bacteria in fresh yoghurt keep our digestive system in good shape. These foods and many more are called functional foods.

Food companies develop artificially functional foods too. Sometimes they add vitamins or minerals to foods that don't have these nutrients

Transplanting Genes

Some functional foods are genetically modified organisms (GMOs). To create a GMO, scientists put a gene from one organism (living thing) into another. This gives the new organism a trait that improves it. One GMO is a rice plant with a corn gene that produces vitamin A. Scientists are also developing soyabeans with genes that produce omega-3 fatty acids.

Flavour scientists are using GMOs to create natural fruit flavourings. They find the genes that give a ripe fruit its flavour. They put the genes into bacteria. The scientists then use those bacteria to make large amounts of the fruit's flavour chemicals. One day your porridge may be flavoured by bacteria.

Super Foods or Super Problems?

Are GMOs safe to eat? No one knows for sure. Supporters say no scientific evidence shows that GMOs harm people. We've been eating GMOs such as soyabeans and sweet corn for years.

Others say that GMOs may already be making people ill, but we have no way of tracing problems to specific foods. They say mixing genes from different kinds of organisms is risky and unnecessary. They encourage us instead to preserve our planet's biodiversity. The greater its variety of plants and animals, the better chance our food supply has of surviving specific weather stresses, pests, disasters and other problems.

This scientist is extracting a sweet corn embryo. She will use it to develop a GMO sweet corn crop.

naturally. Sometimes they add other nutrients. For example, you may find omega-3 fish oil in your cereal or helpful bacteria in your cheese.

A Swedish company has even developed a drinking straw that releases helpful bacteria. Why doesn't the company just put the bacteria in drinks? Because processing drinks usually takes heat and heat kills the bacteria. A bacteria-lined straw makes any cold drink a functional food.

Tiny Taste Tools

Adding health-boosting chemicals can change a food's taste. Food companies are hoping to solve this problem with nanotechnology. Nanotechnology is making and using tiny tools.

Nanotools are so tiny that people can see them only with superstrong microscopes. Scientists build nanotools with atoms and molecules. Atoms are the bits of matter that make up molecules.

IT'S A FACT!

A nanometre is one-billionth of a metre. Look at a ruler and imagine 10 million points in the space of 1 centimetre. Each

Fruit juice enriched with omega-3 fish

kill the germs with heat. Nanostrainers could even remove the lactose molecules from milk. Lactose is the milk sugar that many people can't digest.

For the Time Being

By 2030 nutrigenomics and nanocuisine may no longer be science fiction. Scientists are working hard to learn about food-gene connections. Others are investigating the safety of nanotools in food.

What should you do in the meantime? Eat natural, healthful, functional foods! If you eat such foods, your high-tech future eating plan may not differ much from your low-tech current diet.

Glossary

aroma: smell

aroma molecules: the parts of a chemical that provide its smell

atoms: the basic building blocks of matter

bacteria: single-celled living things, sometimes called germs

cells: the tiny building blocks that make up living things

digestive system: the group of body parts that break down food so the body can use it

fossil fuel: fuel (such as oil, coal or natural gas) formed underground from decayed ancient plants and animals

genes: tiny chemical bundles inside all cells that tell cells how to keep the body working

genetically modified organism (GMO): an organism created when a scientist takes a gene from one organism and puts it into another kind of organism

genome: the whole set of an organism's genes

molecule: the smallest possible portion of a substance that has all the features of that substance

nanotechnology: a new scientific field that involves creating things on an ultra-small scale by moving individual atoms and molecules

nutrient: a chemical in food that the body needs to grow and be healthy

organisms: living things

primary tastes: basic tastes that combine to make all other tastes

receptor: part of a cell that recognizes and attaches to a specific chemical

Selected Bibliography

Decker, Kimberly J. 'Cut the Calories, Keep the Flavour.' *Food Product Design*. 7 November 2006. http://www.foodproductdesign.com/articles/691concepts.html (27 September 2007).

Barham, Peter. *The Science of Cooking*. New York: Springer, 2001.

Clydesdale, Fergus. 'Functional Foods: Opportunities and Challenges.' *Food Technology*, December 2004, 35-40.

Cowart, Beverly J. 'Taste, Our Body's Gustatory Gatekeeper.' *Cerebrum*, Spring 2005, 7–22.

Fisher, Len. *How to Dunk a Doughnut: The Science of Everyday Life*. London: Weidenfeld and Nicolson, 2002.

Lister, Ted and Heston Blumenthal. *Kitchen Chemistry*. London: Royal Society of Chemistry, 2005.

McGee, Harold. *On Food and Cooking: The Science and Lore of the Kitchen*. New York: Simon and Schuster, 1997.

Nestle, Marion. *What to Eat*. New York: North Point Press, 2006.

Parsons, Russ. *How to Read a French Fry: And Other Stories of Intriguing Kitchen Science*. New York: Houghton Mifflin, 2001.

Pollan, Michael. *The Omnivore's Dilemma: A Natural History of Four Meals*. New York: Penguin, 2006.

This, Hervé. *Molecular Gastronomy: Exploring the Science of Flavour*. New York: Columbia University Press, 2006.

Wolke, Robert L. *What Einstein Told His Cook: Kitchen Science Explained*. New York: W W Norton and Company, 2002.

Further Reading and Websites

Ballard, Carol. *How Do We Taste and Smell?* (How Our Bodies Work) Hodder
    Wayland, 2001.

Bowden, Rob. *Food and Farming* (Sustainable World) Hodder Wayland, 2007.

Bramwell, Martyn and Catriona Lennox. *Food Watch* Dorling Kindersley, 2001.

Dagleish, Sharon. *Healthy Choices Fast Food* Nelson Thornes, 2008.

Famdon, Jon. *From DNA to GM Wheat: Discovering Genetically Modified* (Chain
    Reactions) Heinemann, 2007.

Fridell, Ron. *Genetic Engineering* Lerner Publishing Group, Inc., 2008.

Ganeri, Anita. *Senses* (How My Body Works) Evans Brothers Ltd., 2006

Johnson, Rebecca L. *Nanotechnology*. Lerner Publishing Group, Inc., 2008.

Jones, Carol. *Pasta and Noodles* (From Farm to You) Nelson Thornes, 2008.

Mayer, Cassie. *Farming* (Our Global Community) Heinemann, 2007.

Spilsbury, Louise. *Food and Agriculture: How We Use the Land* Heinemann, 2006.

Suhr, Mandy and Mike Gordon. *Taste* (Senses) Hodder Wayland, 2007.

Thompson, R. *Farming* (Changing Times) Franklin Watts, Ltd., 2004.

The Accidental Scientist: Science of Cooking

    http://www.exploratorium.edu/cooking/index.html

    This website explains the science behind food and cooking.

Nanooze

    http://www.nanooze.org.

    This website explains recent discoveries in science and technology – especially
    nanotechnology.

Science News for Kids

    http://www.sciencenewsforkids.org

    This website's 'Food and Nutrition' section provides constantly updated news on
    what we eat – and what we may be eating in the future.

http://www.face-online.org.uk/

This website has loads of information about farming, biodiversity, healthy living and organic food production. It even includes a 'CowCam' which gives you a look at being in a dairy farm from the eyes of the cow! The site also has loads of other activities for children as well as an image and video gallery.

Index

Photo Acknowledgements

The images in this book are used with the permission of: © Comstock Images, all backgrounds, pp 1, 10, 17 (bottom); © J Silver/SuperStock, p 5; © John Shipes/StockFood/Getty Images, p 6; © William Radcliffe/Science Faction/Getty Images, p 7; USDA Photo, p 9; © iStockphoto.com/Peter Dean, p 11; © Colin Cuthbert/Photo Researchers, Inc., p 12; © Neil Setchfield/Alamy, p 14; © Photodisc/Getty Images, pp 16, 17 (top), 28; © Clive Streeter/Dorling Kindersley/Getty Images, p 19; © Phanie/Photo Researchers, Inc., p 21; Courtesy of Danny Hartmann, p 23 (both); © Roberto Brosan/Time & Life Pictures/Getty Images, p 24; © image100 Ltd./CORBIS, p 27; © Hoang Dinh/AFP/Getty Images, p 33; Brand X Pictures, p 37; © Sam Ogden/Photo Researchers, Inc., p 38; © Jim Richardson/CORBIS, p 40.

Front cover: © Zomi/Stone/Getty Images (bottom); © Colin Cuthbert/Photo Researchers, Inc. (center); © iStockphoto.com/Nick Garrad (top left); USDA Photo (top right); © Comstock Images (background). Back cover: © Comstock Images.

Text copyright © 2009 by Jeanne Miller

First published in the United States of America in 2009

About the Author

Jeanne Miller has been writing on science topics for young readers for more than ten years. Her articles have appeared in *Odyssey*, *Cricket*, *AppleSeeds* and elsewhere. She lives in Berkeley, California, USA.